Read for a
Better World™

OUR LEADERS
A First Look

PERCY LEED

GRL Consultant, Diane Craig, Certified Literacy Specialist

Lerner Publications ◆ Minneapolis

Educator Toolbox

Reading books is a great way for kids to express what they're interested in. Before reading this title, ask the reader these questions:

What do you think this book is about? Look at the cover for clues.

What do you already know about leaders?

What do you want to learn about leaders?

Let's Read Together

Encourage the reader to use the pictures to understand the text.

Point out when the reader successfully sounds out a word.

Praise the reader for recognizing sight words such as *to* and *for*.

TABLE OF CONTENTS

Our Leaders 4

Our Leaders

We need leaders.
A leader is the person
in charge.

Some people choose
to be leaders.

Parents are the leaders of a family.

A teacher is the leader of a class.

A coach is the leader of a team.

**What other groups
need leaders?**

We choose some leaders.

Have you ever voted for something?

We vote for them.

Our leaders work together.

They work with leaders from other places too.

Our leaders make rules.
Good leaders make
things fair and safe
for all of us.

Good leaders care about
the people they lead.

They work to make
our lives better.

What else
makes a good
leader?

How can you be a leader?

You Connect!

What is something you would like about being a leader?

What can you do to be a leader at school?

Who are some leaders you know?

Social and Emotional Snapshot

Student voice is crucial to building reader confidence. Ask the reader:

What is your favorite part of this book?

What is something you learned from this book?

Did this book remind you of any leaders you know?

Photo Glossary

coach

parents

teacher

vote

Learn More

Bolinder, Mary Kate. *Presidents*. Huntington Beach, CA: Teacher Created Materials, 2022.

Redford, Ruth. *Great Leaders*. New York: DK Publishing, 2020.

Stratton, Connor. *State Governments*. Lake Elmo, MN: Focus Readers, 2024.

Index

Photo Acknowledgments

The images in this book are used with the permission of: © SDI Productions/iStockphoto, pp. 4–5; © omgimages/iStockphoto, p. 6; © kate_sept2004/iStockphoto, pp. 7, 23; © WavebreakMediaMicro/Adobe Stock, pp. 8–9, 23; © Monkey Business Images/Shutterstock Images, pp. 10–11, 20, 23; © wavebreak3/Adobe Stock, p. 12; © rawpixel.com/Teddy Rawpixel/Adobe Stock, pp. 13, 23; © Ground Picture/Shutterstock Images, pp. 14, 19; © Chokniti-Studio/Shutterstock Images, p. 15; © AnnaStills/Adobe Stock, pp. 16–17; © Drazen Zigic/iStockphoto, p. 18.

Cover Photograph: © Nina/peopleimages.com/Adobe Stock

Design Elements: © Mighty Media, Inc.

Lerner Publications Company
An imprint of Lerner Publishing Group, Inc.
241 First Avenue North
Minneapolis, MN 55401 USA

For reading levels and more information, look up this title at www.lernerbooks.com.

Main body text set in Mikado a Medium.
Typeface provided by Hannes von Doehren.

Library of Congress Cataloging-in-Publication Data

Names: Leed, Percy, 1968–author.
Title: Our leaders : a first look / Percy Leed.
Description: Minneapolis : Lerner Publications, 2024. | Series: Read for a better world. Read about citizenship | Includes bibliographical references and index. | Audience: Ages 5–8 | Audience: Grades K–1 | Summary: "Leaders can be all sorts of people, like your teacher or your coach. They help us to be good citizens. Full-color photographs and easy-to-read text help readers understand why leaders are important"—Provided by publisher.
Identifiers: LCCN 2023012206 (print) | LCCN 2023012207 (ebook) | ISBN 9798765608739 (library binding) | ISBN 9798765624623 (paperback) | ISBN 9798765616581 (epub)
Subjects: LCSH: Civic leaders—Juvenile literature. | Citizenship—Juvenile literature.
Classification: LCC HN42 .L44 2024 (print) | LCC HN42 (ebook) | DDC 303.3/4—dc23/eng/20230426

LC record available at https://lccn.loc.gov/2023012206
LC ebook record available at https://lccn.loc.gov/2023012207

Manufactured in the United States of America
1 – CG – 12/15/23